AMERICAN PRESIDENTS

BARACK OBAMA

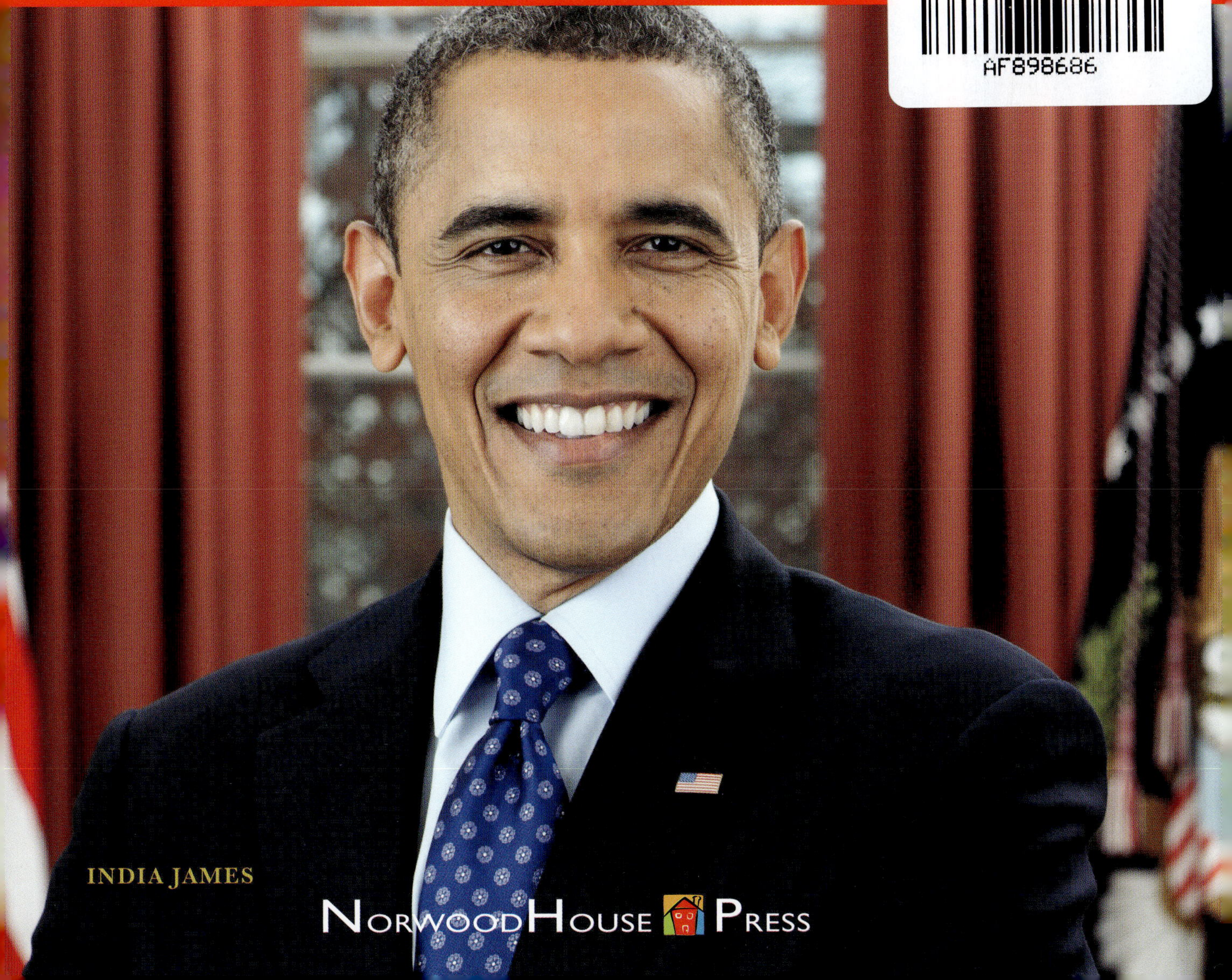

INDIA JAMES

NorwoodHouse Press

Cataloging-in-Publication Data

Names: James, India.
Title: Barack Obama / India James.
Description: Buffalo, NY : Norwood House Press, 2027. | Series: American presidents | Includes glossary and index.
Identifiers: ISBN 9781978579729 (pbk.) | ISBN 9781978579736 (library bound) | ISBN 9781978579743 (ebook)
Subjects: LCSH: Obama, Barack--Juvenile literature. | Presidents--United States--Biography--Juvenile literature. | African American politicians--Biography--Juvenile literature. | Politicians--United States--Biography--Juvenile literature.
Classification: LCC E908. J36 2027 | DDC 973.932092--dc23

Published in 2027 by
Norwood House Press
2544 Clinton Street
Buffalo, NY 14224

Designer: Rhea Magaro
Editor: Kim Thompson

Photo credits: Cover, pp. 1, 11 The White House; p. 4 Efired/Shutterstock.com; p. 5 Terelyuk/Shutterstock.com; p. 7 wavebreakmedia/Shutterstock.com; p. 8 AindriuH/Shutterstock.com; p. 9 Annie Leibovitz; p. 10 AnnaStills/Shutterstock.com; p. 12 MSgt Cecilio Ricardo; p. 13 ara kripik/Shutterstock.com; p. 14 Vitalii Vodolazskyi/Shutterstock.com; pp. 17, 21 Wikipedia; p. 19 Drazen Zigic/Shutterstock.com; p. 20 Peter Serocki/Shutterstock.com;

Printed in the United States of America

Some of the images in this book illustrate individuals who are models. The depictions do not imply actual situations or events.

CPSIA compliance information: Batch #CSNHP27: For further information contact Norwood House Press at 1-800-237-9932.

TABLE OF CONTENTS

Early Years

Barack Obama was born on August 4, 1961, in Honolulu, Hawaii. Then, he moved to **Indonesia**. He lived there as a young child with his mother and stepfather.

When he was in fifth grade, Barack went back to Hawaii. He moved in with his grandparents.

Barack was a good student, but he did not have the best grades in his class. He liked playing basketball. He was on the **varsity** team at his high school.

Building a Career

Barack attended Columbia University in New York City. After graduation, he started work in Chicago, Illinois. His job was to help people in poor areas of the city. Later, he went to law school at Harvard University before returning to Chicago.

Chicago

In 1992, Barack married Michelle Robinson.

They had two daughters, Malia and Sasha.

Barack thought it was important for people to vote. He started Project Vote, an organization that helped thousands of people register to vote.

People liked what Barack was doing. In 2004, they elected him to the United States **Senate** to represent the state of Illinois.

Presidency

Barack was elected as the 44th president of the U.S. in 2008. He was the first African American person to become president.

The country was in the Great **Recession**. It was a difficult time. Many people did not have jobs. Barack created programs to help workers across the country.

Affordable Care Act

Barack believed that everyone should be able to see a doctor when they are sick. He wanted all Americans to have health **insurance**. He created the Affordable Care Act, which is often called Obamacare. It helped people pay for doctor and hospital visits.

When Barack was president, the U.S. was fighting with Iraq, Afghanistan, and other nations. Barack worked hard to bring peace. He visited the countries to improve relations. For his efforts, Barack was awarded the **Nobel Peace Prize** in 2009.

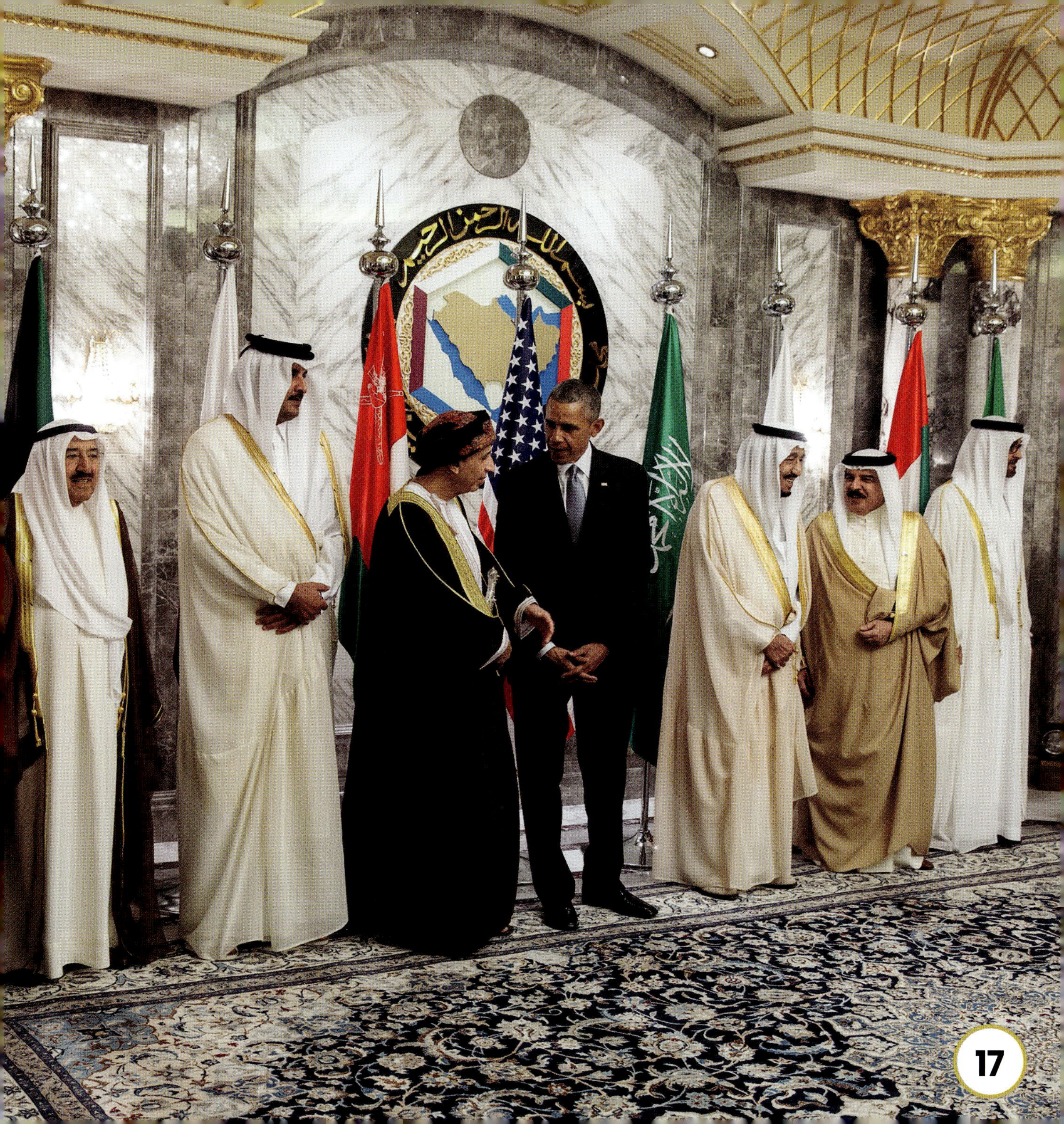

Later Life

Barack served two **terms** as president. After leaving the White House, he and Michelle stayed in Washington, D.C. They started the Obama Foundation to help young people become leaders in their communities.

Barack is still active in **politics**. He works to help people get elected. He gives speeches around the world.

Barack Obama is remembered as a popular and caring president. He helped make the world healthier and more peaceful.

Glossary

Indonesia (in-duh-NEE-zhuh): a country in Southeast Asia, north of Australia

insurance (in-SHOOR-uhns): a system in which people pay money to a company that agrees to pay for doctors, hospitals, home repairs, or other necessary services

Nobel Peace Prize (noh-BEL pees prize): a global award given each year to someone who makes the world more peaceful

politics (PAH-li-tiks): participation in government

recession (ri-SESH-uhn): a time when business slows down and many people lose their jobs

Senate (SEN-it): one half of the U.S. Congress; a body elected to make laws that includes two senators from each U.S. state

terms (turmz): definite or set periods of time; American presidents are elected to terms that last four years

varsity (VAHR-suh-tee): the highest level of sports in high school

Thinking Questions

1. Where did Barack live when he was growing up?

2. What job did Barack have before he became president?

3. How did Barack help people during the Great Recession?

4. What did the Affordable Care Act do?

5. What award did Barack Obama win in 2009?

Index

About the Author

India James writes about science, technology, math, and history for young readers. She loves learning new things while writing books. India lives in Ohio with her family.